# MAKING KITES

# MAKING
# KITES

## How to build and fly your very own kites - from simple sleds to complex stunters

RHODA BAKER & MILES DENYER

THE
APPLE
PRESS

A QUINTET BOOK

Published by The Apple Press
6 Blundell Street
London N7 9BH

ISBN 1-85076-366-6

This book was designed and produced by
Quintet Publishing Limited
6 Blundell Street
London N7 9BH

Creative Director: Richard Dewing
Designer: Pete Laws
Project Editors: Bill Hemsley/Katie Preston
Editor: Jenny Millington
Photographer: Jeremy Thomas

Typeset in Great Britain by
Central Southern Typesetters, Eastbourne
Manufactured in Singapore by
Eray Scan Pte Limited
Printed in Hong Kong by
Leefung-Asco Printers Limited

**Acknowledgements**
The Publishers would also like to thank Gill Bloom for
supplying the pictures on pages 7, 9 and 21 and the
Ann Ronan Picture Library at Image Select for
supplying the pictures on page 11.

# CONTENTS

# INTRODUCTION

# THE EARLY HISTORY OF KITES

Kites originated in Asia and were probably invented in China about 3,000 years ago. Kite flying may also have developed independently among the islands of Micronesia in the South Pacific. From China, the secret of kite building quickly spread to Korea, Japan, Malaysia and India, countries where kites are still very popular today.

It is unclear when kites first appeared in Europe, but they may have been known to the ancient Greeks. They were certainly in use by the time of the Battle of Hastings in 1066, when strings of kites were flown as battle signals. The English name – kite – is taken from the kite, a graceful bird of prey.

## RITUAL

In Asia, kites have often had a ritual or religious significance. Many Chinese kites were built to represent the dragons of Chinese folklore. Other traditional designs include birds, butterflies and even centipedes.

In Malaysia, kites flying over a house at night are believed to keep away evil spirits. In Korea, the name of a new-born child is often inscribed on a kite, which is then released to the wind. The Koreans believe that the kite carries with it any evil spirits that attended the child's birth. To find such a kite is thought to bring bad luck.

In Japan, the inhabitants of a village often co-operated to build one huge kite. These village kites measured up to 120 square yards/100 square metres in surface area, and could be flown only at festivals because they needed all the villagers to launch them.

## SPORT

Kites were also used for sport, and kite-fighting is still very popular, especially in India and Thailand. Indian fighting kites have powdered glass glued to the line. The idea is to use the glass to cut through the line of an opponent's kite.

In Thailand, kite-fighting is a team sport. Contests take place between one large, star-shaped *chula* kite, and several smaller, diamond-shaped *pakpao* kites. The aim is to entangle an opposing kite and drag it to the ground. As well as providing entertainment, these contests are supposed to make the rainy monsoon winds blow away.

Kite-fighting has also become popular in several South American countries. Razor-blades are attached to the framework of the kite and contestants try to batter and slash each others' kites in mid-air.

## WARFARE

The peoples of Asia soon realized that kites produce considerable "lift", and could be used for carrying ropes across rivers when building a bridge. Large kites could even lift humans, which meant that they could be used in warfare.

As early as 169 BC a Chinese general is said to have sent soldiers aloft on kites to observe a besieged city and estimate the length of tunnel needed to reach the city walls. Old Japanese prints show archers suspended from kites shooting down at the enemy beneath.

Kites had even more sinister uses. The 13th-century traveller Marco Polo relates how Chinese sea-captains would send a prisoner aloft on a kite when trying to decide whether to set sail. If the prisoner was safely returned to earth, then the omens for the voyage were good. If, however, the prisoner failed to survive, the voyage was postponed. Fortunately, this method of weather forecasting has since been superseded.

## AERIAL ARTISTS?

The Nazca people of ancient Peru carved a great network of lines and pictures into the flat desert landscape. Most of the pictures are so big that they cannot be appreciated from the ground. The designs make sense only when viewed from the air. The pictures have puzzled scientists ever since they were discovered. Some people have claimed that the work was carried out by visitors from outer space. Another theory suggests that the pictures were designed by artist-priests suspended from kites, although there is no other evidence of kite flying in South America at this time. It is otherwise accepted that kites did not reach America until after its "discovery" by Europeans in 1492.

**Above**

*Kites, like those shown, flying in train can reach spectacular heights.*

**Left**

*A modern kite which uses a traditional Asian motif and design.*

# LATER DEVELOPMENTS

In Europe kites became children's playthings, but they did not attract serious attention until the 18th century. In 1749 the Scottish scientist Alexander Wilson used a series of kites with thermometers attached to measure the air temperature at different altitudes.

Three years later, in 1752, the American Benjamin Franklin carried out his famous experiment to prove that lightning was electricity. By flying a kite during a thunderstorm, he showed that electricity passed down the string, when he received a shock from a key attached to the lower end. In fact, Franklin was extremely lucky to survive because this was a very dangerous experiment. The electricity from the lightning could quite easily have killed him.

Kites continued to be used for exploring the atmosphere until the early 20th century, when they were superseded by balloons, airplanes and, eventually, satellites.

## IDEA OF FLIGHT

In 1804, after flying a kite with a curved surface, the Englishman Sir George Cayley developed the idea of untethered heavier-than-air flight. Later he built a large, kite-shaped glider that succeeded in carrying his servant across a valley.

At the end of the 19th century, the Americans Wilbur and Orville Wright used kites to test their ideas for a flying machine. In 1903 they made the first ever powered flight.

Meanwhile, tethered kite flights had become all the rage in Europe and America, and were a popular attraction at fairs and shows. The Anglo-American Samuel Cody, a flamboyant showman, used kites to tow himself across the English Channel.

The inventor of the telephone, Alexander Graham Bell, also designed a tetrahedronal kite made of pyramid-shaped cells. In 1907 one of his kites (containing 3,393 individual cells) lifted a man to a height of 170 feet/50 metres when towed behind a small steamship.

## PRACTICAL PURPOSES

Beyond the idea of flight itself, kites also had a number of other practical (and not so practical) uses.

In 1827 the Englishman George Pocock used a pair of large kites to tow a wheeled carriage, or "flying chariot". For quite obvious reasons, the idea never caught on. In 1847 a child's kite was used during the construction of a suspension bridge across the Niagara River in the United States.

The Italian Guglielmo Marconi used a kite to lift an aerial high enough for him to receive the first transatlantic radio signal in 1901. Five years later, kites were used to take aerial photographs of the damage caused by the 1906 San Francisco earthquake.

In 1919 a train of eight kites flown from Germany reached an altitude of nearly 6½ miles/10,000 metres. An early science-fiction writer even suggested that kites could be used to carry people to the moon!

## THE SECOND WORLD WAR

During the Second World War, kites were used for a variety of different purposes: as observation platforms towed behind ships and submarines; as targets for training anti-aircraft gunners; and as part of the survival pack for aircrew who went down at sea. The *Gibson Girl* kite hoisted a radio aerial so that a distress message could be transmitted.

## AEROBATIC KITES

Since the Second World War, there has been a resurgence of interest in kite-flying just for the fun of it. This interest has been stimulated by the introduction of new kite designs that can perform controlled aerobatic manoeuvres.

In 1948 Francis Rogallo patented his Flexi-wing kite, which was also the forerunner of the modern hang-glider and microlight aircraft.

Domina Jalbert designed the aerodynamic parafoil in 1964; this can be used both as a kite and as a parachute. Parafoiling behind speedboats has become a popular attraction at beach resorts.

In 1975 Peter Powell introduced his dual-line stunt kite, which opened up a whole new world of high-excitement stunt-kiting.

**Left**

*The American Woodbridge Davis devised a kite in 1894 for reaching shipwrecks. The kite carried a rescue line which was used to bring a breeches-buoy to the survivors.*

**Below**

*In Switzerland in 1844, Dr Colladon was also investigating the lifting power of the kite. A dummy, sitting in a wicker chair, was blown along a kite line by means of a large umbrella.*

# FLYING A
# SINGLE-LINE
# KITE

Select a suitable open flying area clear of obstructions and buildings that can create air turbulence. Smooth launching requires a steady air-flow. If flying on a hillside, choose the windward side of the hill.

Check that your kite is correctly assembled – that the struts are secure; that the bridle is properly positioned for flying; that the tail (if fitted) is unfurled; and that the line is not tangled.

## LAUNCHING

The worst way to launch a kite is to run with it. If the wind has moderate speed, then it is easy to self-launch a kite.

Stand with your back to the wind, with the handle in one hand and the kite in the other. Hold the kite up at arm's length and release it, unwinding some line as you do so. Let out more line as the kite rises.

In light winds, you may need a helper to assist you with a long-launch. With your back to the wind, ask the helper to take the kite and walk backwards for 30–50ft/10–15 metres. Unwind line as he or she does so. At your signal, the helper should release the kite, while you pull in some line to help the kite to rise.

## FLYING TIPS

If the kite has difficulty gaining height, you can winch it up. Allow some line out, so that the kite falls. Just before it touches the ground, quickly reel in the line causing the kite to climb. Repeat this until the kite has sufficient altitude.

If the kite suddenly starts to dive, don't panic and don't pull. Let out more line, and the kite will probably right itself. To avoid crashing your kite, release the handle and line about a yard/1 metre before it hits the ground to give a softer landing.

If the lines of two kites cross, don't pull. Both fliers should walk towards each other until the lines uncross.

The standard way to land a kite, is to pull in all the line with both hands, making sure a tangle does not form at your feet. With large and hard-pulling kites, you may need to walk the kite down, running a gloved hand along the line.

**Right**
*To self launch a kite hold the kite vertically by the bottom edge and release it, letting out a little line.*

*If self launching isn't successful, try a long launch. Give the signal to release the kite and either move backwards or pull the line in.*

12

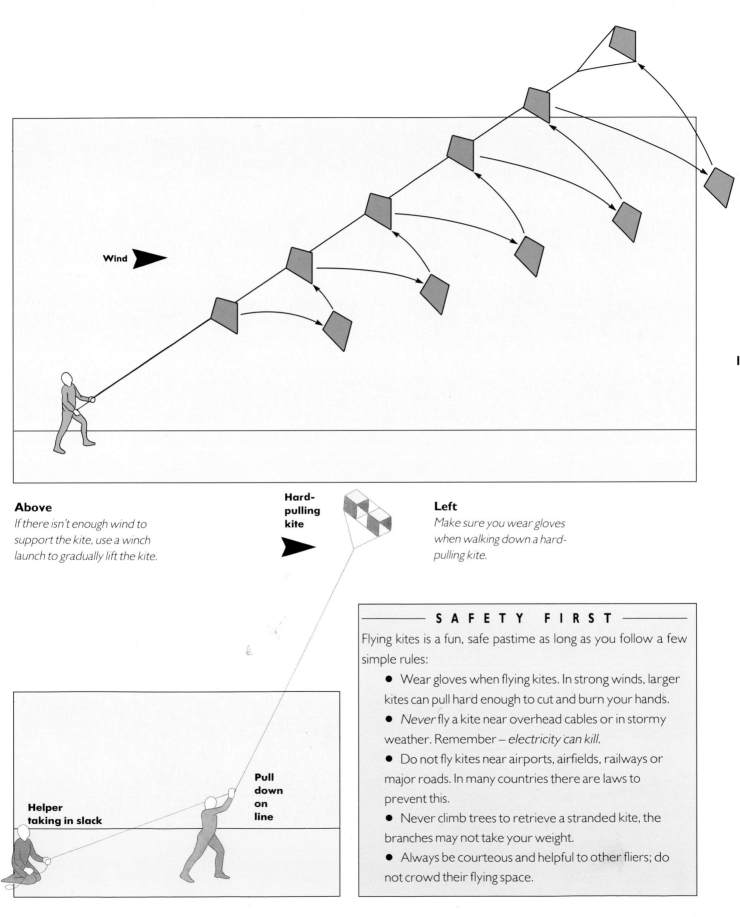

**Above**
*If there isn't enough wind to support the kite, use a winch launch to gradually lift the kite.*

**Wind**

**Hard-pulling kite**

**Left**
*Make sure you wear gloves when walking down a hard-pulling kite.*

**Helper taking in slack**

**Pull down on line**

---

### SAFETY FIRST

Flying kites is a fun, safe pastime as long as you follow a few simple rules:

- Wear gloves when flying kites. In strong winds, larger kites can pull hard enough to cut and burn your hands.
- *Never* fly a kite near overhead cables or in stormy weather. Remember – *electricity can kill.*
- Do not fly kites near airports, airfields, railways or major roads. In many countries there are laws to prevent this.
- Never climb trees to retrieve a stranded kite, the branches may not take your weight.
- Always be courteous and helpful to other fliers; do not crowd their flying space.

# FLYING A DUAL-LINE STUNT KITE

Unlike a single-line kite, a stunt kite will not stay airborne by itself. Stunt kites need constant attention and control to keep them aloft. Basic control is very simple – you hold one line-handle in each hand; pull on the left-hand line to move the kite to the left, and pull on the right to move right.

Stunt kites can swoop at speeds over 60mph/100kph and can therefore be dangerous. Take the greatest care not to hit other fliers or bystanders. If you doubt whether there is enough room to fly your stunt kite, find a larger and more open space.

## LAUNCHING

With practice, you can self-launch a stunt kite, but beginners will find it easier with the assistance of a helper. Remember always to keep the wind behind you.

Ask the helper to walk the kite backwards while you unwind the lines. Make sure that they are the same length and do not become crossed or tangled. At your signal, the helper should lift the kite and release it, while you step backwards and pull the kite up into the air. Keep your hands together as the kite rises.

At first, let the kite rise as high as it can and practise basic control. To fly straight, keep both hands together.

## FLYING TIPS

The shorter your lines, the faster your reactions have to be in order to keep control. For beginners, lines about 200ft/60 metres long will give enough reaction time for practising.

While practising, keep your kite away from the ground, otherwise it may crash and be damaged.

Stunt kites tend to speed up when they near the ground – step forwards and slacken the lines in order to reduce speed.

## AERIAL MANOEUVRES

The simplest manoeuvre is the loop, performed by gently moving one hand back, pulling on one line. Start with large loops, keeping your hands close together. Smaller loops are made with the hands further apart. After performing loops in one direction, uncross the lines with an equal number of loops in the other direction.

Other simple manoeuvres include the vertical figure-of-eight and the power dive.

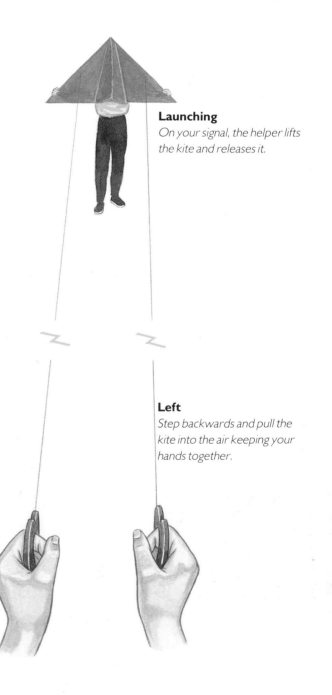

**Launching**
*On your signal, the helper lifts the kite and releases it.*

**Left**
*Step backwards and pull the kite into the air keeping your hands together.*

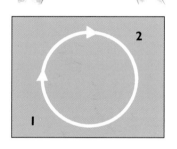

**Right turn**

*Gently pull on the right-hand line to steer to the right.*

**Left turn**

*Gently pull on the left-hand line to steer to the left.*

**Simple loop**

*1 Pull back gently on the right-hand line to make the kite loop.*

*2 At the peak of the loop bring your hands level.*

**Figure-of-eight**

*1 Pull the right-hand line back and then forwards again so that your hands are level.*

*2 Pull the left-hand line back and then bring your hands level.*

*3 Pull your right-hand line back gently to return to the beginning.*

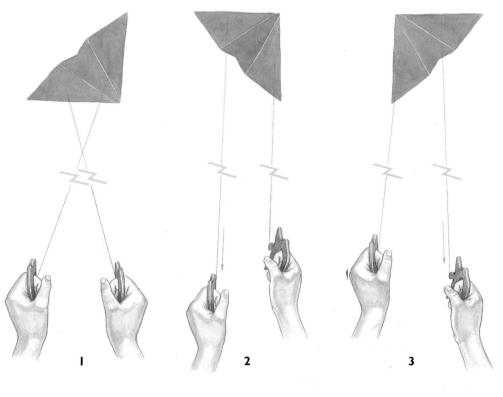

# MATERIALS
# AND
# EQUIPMENT

We have suggested suitable materials for each of the kites in this book, but these can usually be varied depending on your resources – financial or otherwise! Specialist kite shops will stock wonderful, but more expensive, items – with imagination, these can often be replaced with cheaper substitutes, and the kites will fly just as well. Kites made from alternative materials are best tested in calmer wind conditions – experiment and have fun!

## FABRIC, PLASTIC AND PAPER

Ripstop nylon is the ideal kite-making fabric, being very strong and colourful, but it is expensive and can be hard to find unless you have a kite shop locally. Kites can be made just as effectively from any strong fabric that doesn't stretch too much, such as cotton, polyester or even silk.

The simpler kites can be made from sheet plastic, which could be a black or green bin liner cut to shape, or even a supermarket carrier bag – a good way to recycle them! Many kites can also be made of ordinary wrapping paper, tissue paper, or even newspaper, and will survive for a surprisingly long time, unless they get wet.

## SPARS AND FRAMES

Dowel makes a good light frame and is inexpensive – choose ramin hardwood dowel for strength. Kite shops will sell the more hi-tech materials such as fibreglass or carbon fibre rods, which will be needed for the stunt kites in this book. Small, lightweight kites may need only a split bamboo or even a drinking-straw frame to fly successfully.

## LINES AND KNOTS

There are many different kinds and weights of kite lines available – the best are the braided lines, with twisted lines a cheaper alternative. Most are made from nylon or polyester. The smaller kites can be flown from ordinary thread or light string.

Four different types of handles and reels.

A handle for a lightweight kite need only be plywood with a notch at each end.
A simple shape like this can be cut from plywood with a jig saw, and makes a very good handle and line reel all in one.

## HANDLES AND REELS

Again, handles can vary from the expensive, ready-made variety to a simple piece of plywood with a notch at each end to wind the line around. Wooden handles are reasonably easy to make, and can be adapted to suit your hand – obviously strength and comfort are most important. Reels and spools for the flying line are not really essential for any of the simpler kites.

16

**Basic equipment**
*(clockwise from top)*
*junior hacksaw*
*marker pens*
*metal ruler*
*sticky tape*
*sandpaper*
*pencils*
*scissors*
*masking tape*
*craft knife*
*needle and thread*
*pins*
*glue stick*
*cutting mat*

## BRIDLES

Some kites will fly with just a simple flying line attached – the Box Kite project in this book is an example. Others need a bridle to provide an attachment point for the flying line and to keep the kite in the correct position in the wind. Adjusting the bridle slightly will tilt the kite against the wind and alter the way it flies.

Lowering the towing point when the wind is light will allow more of the kite's surface to catch the wind. In stronger wind conditions, the kite will need to tilt more towards the horizontal, and will need a higher towing point.

Hang the kite from your finger by the bridle point to check its balance. If one side is noticeably heavier, trim the decorations until both sides are even. Attach the flying line.

## BITS AND PIECES

We have used split rings (like small keyrings) to make the kites described in this book – they are easier to attach to lines and loops than closed, alloy rings, which also cost more. End caps for spars are also available but not essential – we protect the pockets by wrapping the ends of the spars with tape. A trip round any large hardware store will help you to find plastic tubing, dowelling and many small items such as split rings.

## KEELS

The use of a keel in a bridling system gives very good stability. The keel is a triangle made of the same material as the kite, with the longest side along the spine of the kite. A keel bridle blocks the path of the wind and so the kite is laterally stable. Two or three alternative towing points can be made at the bottom tip of the keel, for example in the Diamond Keeled kite, which allow for adjustment in different wind conditions.

As well as stability a keel helps to distribute stress along the whole length of the sail, rather than having stress at the points where the bridle is attached. This means that flight is much more smooth and controlled.

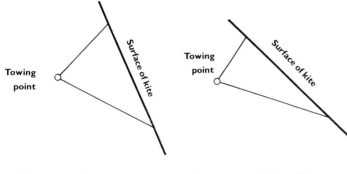

*A lower towing point is needed in light wind conditions.*

*In stronger wind conditions, move the towing point up towards the top of the kite.*

## HINTS FOR CONSTRUCTION

All the kites in this book are reasonably straightforward to make: if you are a beginner, start with the easy projects such as the Paperfold Kite or Sled. Follow the steps slowly, and refer to the picture of the finished kite to see what shape you are aiming for.

## SAFETY FIRST

When cutting out plastic or tubes with craft knives, remember to use a cutting mat or a thick layer of card to protect the surface you are cutting on. *Never* use a craft knife to cut towards yourself or your free hand – if the blade slips you could suffer serious injury. Keep all sharp equipment safely to one side out of the reach of children, and away from areas where you are likely accidentally to lean on blades or points.

## SEWING AND GLUING

Many of the kites in this book can be assembled using just a glue stick – obviously kites that are going to be flown in high winds and used for stunts need stronger construction techniques. Sewn kites can use simple flat seams or the stronger flat fell seam.

## REPAIRS

If you make a mistake during construction, don't despair – usually a repair or patch will be easy to make and won't show at all once the kite is airborne. Make sure any repairs

## SEWING A FLAT FELL SEAM

**1** *Put the right sides of the cloth together and stitch a seam ½in/15mm from the edge.*

**2** *Press the seam open, and trim one side of the seam allowance to half its width.*

**3** *Fold the wider seam allowance over the trimmed edge and sew through all the layers. The resulting seam should always be on the back of the kite.*

will match the rest of the kite for strength. If a patch is applied to one side of a kite it may affect the kite's stability, so keep the two sides symmetrical by applying a matching patch to the other side as well.

Kites made from paper or plastic can be repaired using sticky tape or insulating tape. Fabric kites will often accept sticky tape patches too, or you can use spare pieces of fabric and glue or iron-on interfacing. Ripstop nylon kites can be repaired using special ripstop nylon tape or by sewing on a patch.

If a kite is damaged while flying, simple repairs can be made on the spot with sticky tape, spare pieces of fabric and glue or staples. It might be a good idea to carry a small emergency repair kit with you on flying expeditions just in case. Remember, again, to keep the kite wings symmetrical.

## —— M A K I N G   A   P A T T E R N ——

Where we have used a diagram for the basic parts of the kite, this will need to be scaled up to the finished size of the kite. You will need a large sheet of blank paper to make your pattern. Rule the paper into the same number of squares scaled up from the squares shown in the diagram – for example, 1in/25mm squares in the diagram, scaled up by 200% will mean drawing squares of 2in/50mm on your pattern paper. Using erasable pencil, carefully copy the shape of the kite onto your pattern square by square. You should now have a full-size pattern from which to cut out your material.

## —— K N O T S ——

We recommend three types of knots – each has a different function:

● **OVERHAND KNOT** makes a secure knot for attaching to split rings or around spars.

● **BOWLINE KNOT** is a non-slip knot for attaching lines to spars or handles.

● **LARK'S HEAD KNOT** attaches a line to a ring, and can be slid up and down for adjustment e.g., for a towing point.

THE PROJECTS

# SLED

**DIFFICULTY:** EASY  **WIND:** LIGHT – MEDIUM

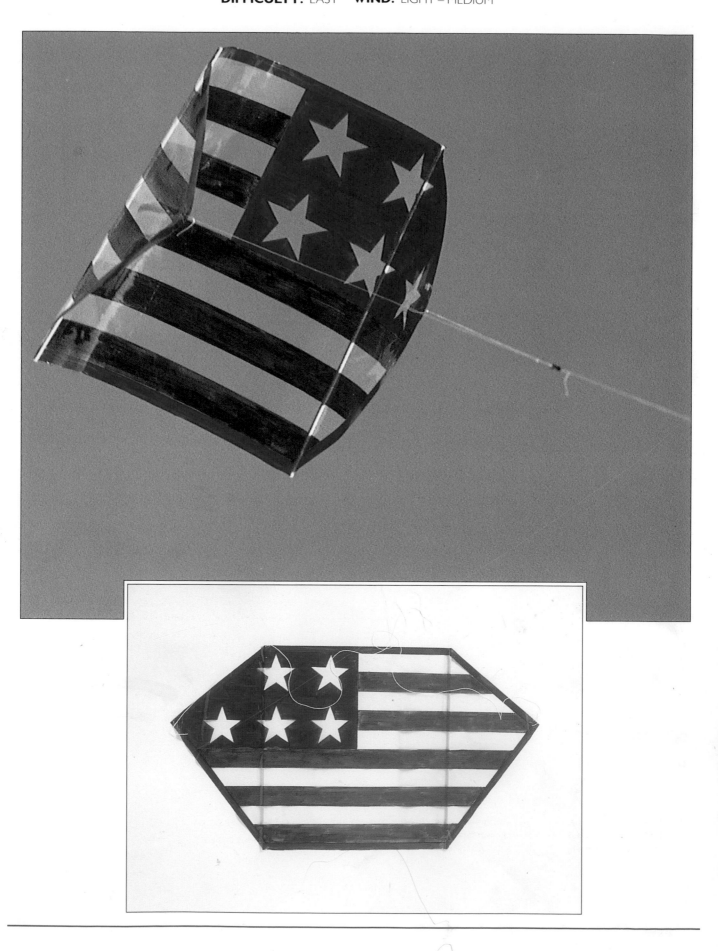

**DIFFICULTY:** EASY  **WIND:** LIGHT – MEDIUM

The sled is a simple kite that is held in shape partly by spars that run along its length and partly by the pressure of the wind, which holds the kite open. The kite needs a long bridle to allow it to open fully. The sled shown here is patterned with what must be the most famous flag in the world, the Stars and Stripes of the United States. The same method may, of course, be used to create other flags or any other pattern you choose.

## MATERIALS

**Sheet plastic or strong plastic bag**

**Two ¼in/4.5mm dowels, both 18in/440mm long**

**Spirit-based marker pens**

**Sticky tape**

**Strong thread**

**Metal ruler and craft knife or scissors**

**Sandpaper (optional)**

**22lb/10kg breaking strain flying line**

## ALTERNATIVE MATERIALS

● **The kite can be made using reasonably strong but flexible paper for the sail. Nylon can also be used.**

## ALTERNATIVE METHODS

● **You can make a scaled-down version of this kite using drinking straws as the spars. Such a kite will fly in light winds.**

● **Two tails may be attached, one to each of the bottom corners of the kite.**

● **Circular vents may be cut in the centre panel of the kite to improve stability. Each hole should be 4in/100mm in diameter. The centre of each hole should be** about 4in/100mm from the bottom edge of the kite and the same distance from the spars.

Double layer of paper

6¼in/160mm

17½in/440mm

11¼in/286mm

8in/200mm

8in/200mm

Fold

**1** *Fold the plastic in half, then mark out the dimensions with a spirit-based felt pen, ensuring that the centre of the kite will be at the fold. Keeping the* material folded, cut out the shape with a craft knife. Use a metal ruler to keep the cuts straight. (Alternatively, you can use a pair of scissors.)

23

**2** *Unfold the plastic and decorate it with spirit-based felt pens (water-based ink will smudge very easily). It may make decorating easier if you hold the plastic in place with sticky tape, but you must be very careful not to damage the plastic when you remove the tape – test the tape on a spare piece of plastic first.*

**3** *Cut the dowels to 18in/ 440mm in length. Smooth the ends using sandpaper. Fix the dowels onto the decorated side of the kite. Each should run from a top to a bottom corner as shown. The dowels are fixed in place with sticky tape at intervals along their length. Reinforce the ends of the dowels with tape stuck over the dowels and round onto the back of the kite.*

**4** *Reinforce the points of the fins with several layers of sticky tape. Pierce holes in the reinforced parts for the bridle. Tie on a 6ft/2m bridle.*

**5** *Tie a loop at the mid-point of the bridle to which to attach the line. Attach the flying line.*

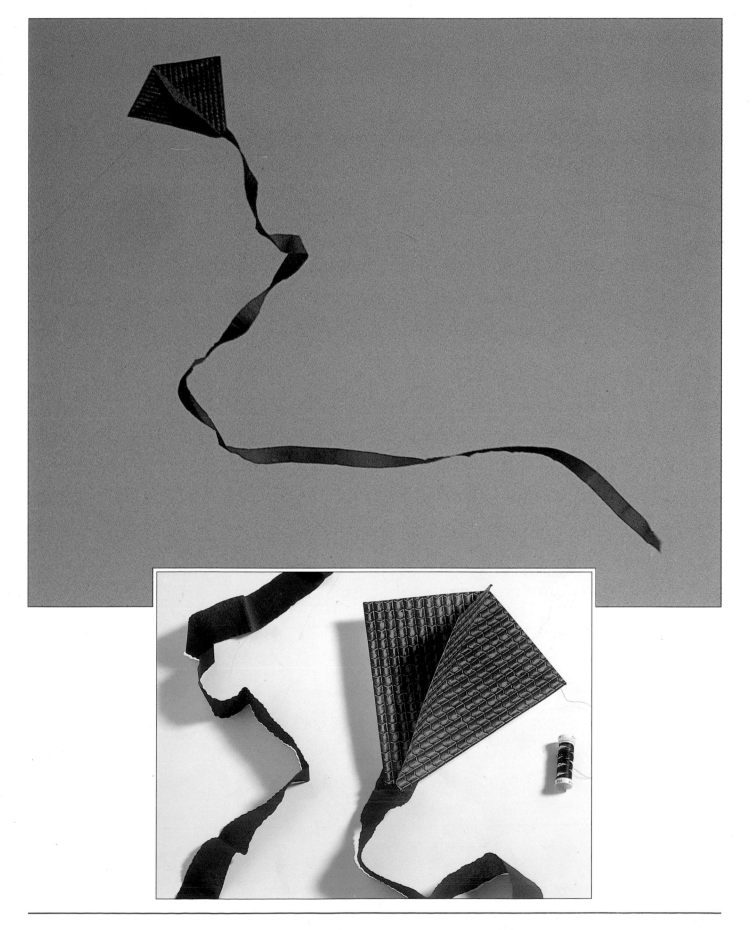

**DIFFICULTY:** EASY **WIND:** LIGHT – MEDIUM

## MATERIALS

**Piece of wrapping paper 8¼in/210mm × 11¾in/300mm (international A4 size)**

**10ft/3.25m length of crepe paper for tail**

**9¼in/235mm lightweight bamboo spar (a bamboo kebab skewer will do)**

**Sticky tape**

**Glue stick**

**Craft knife or scissors**

**Metal ruler**

**Pencil**

**Button thread for flying line**

## ALTERNATIVE MATERIALS

● This kite can be made from any decorated paper, provided it is not too heavy.

● The bamboo spar could be a piece from an old bamboo blind or a split green garden cane.

● The spar could also be made from balsa wood, rattan cane or even a drinking straw.

● The pieces of kite can be fixed together with staples instead of glue.

A kite for beginners! A simple shape that is easy to make and easy to fly as long as the wind is not too strong. If the kite seems to fly erratically, try adding more length to the tail. If the wind gets too strong the kite will be distorted and damaged, so stick to fairly calm days.

**1** *Fold the A4 paper in half with the pattern outwards.*

**2** *With the fold to your right, make a diagonal fold from a point ⅜in/10mm in from the top left and bottom right corners, and fold the flap over. Turn the paper over and make a flap on the other side in the same way.*

**3** Open the paper out and, with the pattern facing you, line up a ruler with the wing tips. Mark the edge of the keel as shown.

**4** Draw a line from the mark to the point at the bottom. Then fold out the lower flap so that it will not be damaged when you cut the keel. Now form the keel by cutting along the line you have drawn.

**5** Glue the sides of the keel together.

**6** Cut a short piece of spar to fit between the points of the wings. Stick the spar to the back of the kite with sticky tape.

**7** Cut a strip of crepe paper 10ft/3.25m long and 1½in/ 40mm wide. Stick one end of the strip onto the bottom of the kite with sticky tape.

**8** Make a hole in the keel, tie on the thread and fly!

**DIFFICULTY:** INTERMEDIATE  **WIND:** MEDIUM – QUITE STRONG

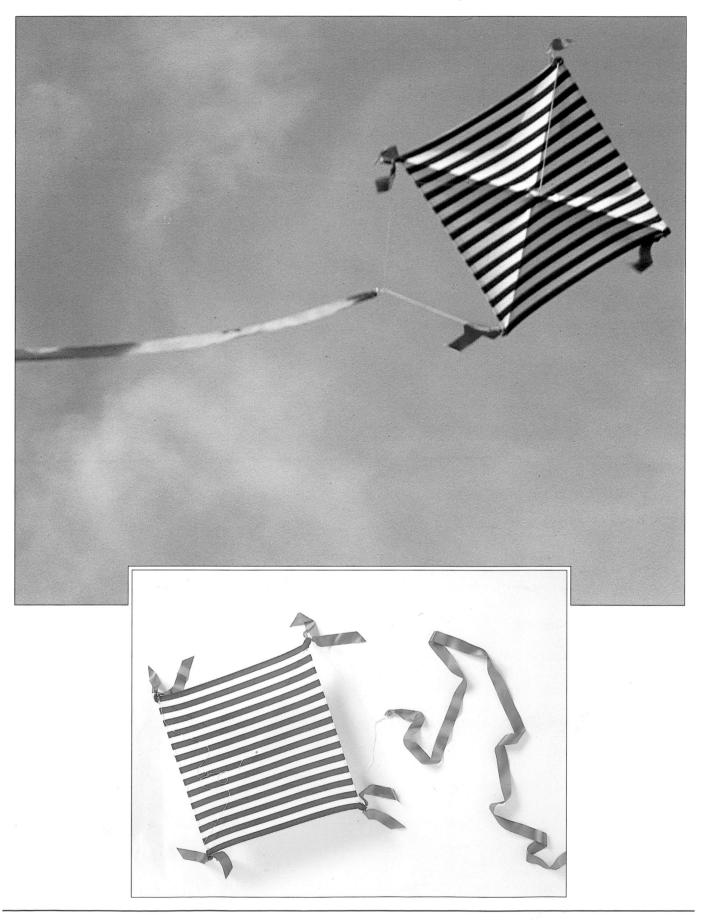

A test flight with this kite will establish whether you need to add length to the tail to improve stability. The angle of flight can also be changed to suit different wind conditions.

### MATERIALS

**Cotton fabric 23in/580mm square**

**About 30ft/10m of 1½in/ 40mm wide ribbon for tail**

**Four pieces of 1½in/40mm wide ribbon, 19in/500mm long (for decoration)**

**Iron-on interfacing, 1⅛in/ 30mm square**

**1in/25mm wide tape or Petersham 16in/400mm long**

**Two pieces of ¼in/6mm dowel, 31in/790mm long**

**Seven ½in/15mm split rings**

**Strong thread**

**Scissors**

**Pencil or tailor's chalk**

**Strong braided line for bridles**

**44lb/20kg flying line**

### ALTERNATIVE MATERIALS

- The dowel used could be a little thinner or thicker without affecting performance.

- The tails and decoration could be made of any cloth offcuts or crepe paper.

- This kite could be made from any cloth that is fairly dense and not liable to stretch too much. If you use a less porous cloth for this kite you may need a stronger flying line.

- Although braided line is better for the bridles, you can use flying line instead.

**1** *Find and mark the centre of the square of fabric by first folding along one diagonal (from corner to corner), then folding the resulting triangle into equal halves so that the opposite corners meet as shown.*

**2** *Cut a small piece of iron-on interfacing and iron it to the back of the fabric at the centre point. Cut a small hole at the centre; this will take one of the lines of the bridle, so it needs to be only about ¼in/6mm in diameter. The edges can be neatened with zigzag stitch if you wish.*

**3** *Make a double fold hem all round the edges of the kite to a depth of about ½in/15mm.*

**Loop of tape**

**Opening of pocket**

**4** To make the pockets, cut four pieces of 1in/25mm wide tape to a length of 4in/100mm each. Fold each piece in half and then fold over about 1in/25mm of the loose ends together as shown.

**5** Stitch the pockets to the back of the kite, placing one at each corner and leaving a loop of tape extending beyond the point to take a split ring, as shown in the diagram.

**6** Thread a split ring onto each loop.

**7** Cut two lengths of dowel about 31in/790mm long. They should fit the kite snugly when they are placed crosswise from corner to corner. Smooth any rough ends with sandpaper. Fit the dowels into the pockets, threading them both through a split ring at the point where they cross.

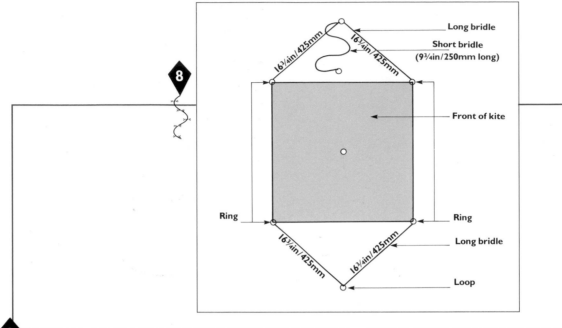

8

Long bridle

Short bridle
(9¾in/250mm long)

16¾in/425mm

16¾in/425mm

Front of kite

Ring

Ring

Long bridle

16¾in/425mm

16¾in/425mm

Loop

9

10

**8** Make the bridles from three lengths of braided line, two pieces 35in/890mm long and one 9¾in/250mm long, each with a loop tied at both ends to thread onto the split rings. The two longer pieces also need a loop tied in the middle. From the front of the kite attach the bridle as shown in the diagram.

**9** Thread the unattached end of short line through the hole in the centre of the kite and attach it to the split ring that joins the dowels.

**10** To make the tail, fold the ribbon in half across its width and stitch a loop at one end. Thread the loop onto a split ring at the centre of the bottom bridle. Decorate the kite with four short lengths of ribbon tied onto the split rings in the corners.

# FIGHTER-STYLE KITE

**DIFFICULTY:** INTERMEDIATE　**WIND:** LIGHT

**DIFFICULTY:** INTERMEDIATE　**WIND:** LIGHT

## MATERIALS

Piece of tissue paper
16in/400mm square

Pieces of tissue paper for
decoration

⅛in/3mm dowel, at least
21in/535mm long

⅛in/3mm cane, at least
24½in/620mm long

Strong thread and a needle

Glue stick

Craft knife or junior
hacksaw

Sandpaper

Scissors

Strong thread for flying
line

## ALTERNATIVE
## MATERIALS

● The kite can also be
made from wrapping
paper or even newspaper!

● The spars are
traditionally made from
split bamboo, which
could be taken from an
old bamboo blind.

34

## STEERING A
## FIGHTING KITE

Fighter kites are
controlled by tightening
and loosening the line.
When the line is taut the
kite flies steadily. To turn
the kite, let out some line
and the kite will rotate in
the air. When the kite is
pointing in the direction
you want, tighten the line
again and the kite will
move in that direction.
Steer the kite by holding
the line, not the reel –
leave the reel and some
spare line lying on the
ground (be careful not to
trip on the loose line). You
will need some practice
before you become skilled
at controlling your kite.

This kite, based on traditional Indian fighter kites, is light and
well-balanced. It can be steered and performs best in a
gentle breeze. The kite should not be flown in damp
conditions because water will weaken or damage the tissue
paper.

**1** *Cut the tissue paper for
the sail to make a 16in/
400mm square.*

**2** *Fold the paper in half
across the diagonal to mark
the position of the spine and
to make sure that both sides
are the same size.*

**3** Decorate the front of the kite with cut-out tissue paper shapes stuck in place with the glue stick. Make the pattern symmetrical to keep the weight even.

**4** Mark two points, one 5⅜in/135mm from each end of the fold on the back of the kite. Stick patches of tissue paper over the points with the glue stick as reinforcement.

**5** Cut the dowel for the spine to 21in/535mm long, and smooth any rough ends with sandpaper. Glue the dowel to the tissue paper at the fold, allowing an equal overlap of tissue paper at each end. Mark the positions of the tissue-reinforced points on the dowel.

**6** Fold in and glue ⅜in/ 10mm of paper along all the edges and over the tips of the spine top and bottom.

**7** *Cut the cane to 24½in/ 620mm long and smooth the ends with sandpaper. Position one end of the cane in an empty corner of the paper, allowing enough overlap to fold over the cane. Glue the cane into the overlap securely.*

**8** *Put a heavy weight on the glued corner, or get someone to hold it down securely. Bend the cane gently and fix the other end into the opposite corner in the same way as you fixed the cane in step 7. The cane should cross the spine at the point that you marked and reinforced earlier.*

**9** *Stick reinforcing patches onto all four corners of the kite to give extra strength. Then cut a length of strong thread and thread the needle. Pierce the paper from front to back with the needle at the reinforced point where the spine and the spar cross. Wind the thread twice around the bowed cane. Return the thread through the paper on the other side of the spine.*

**10** *Knot the thread on the front of the kite. Mark a place 10¼in/260mm along the thread. Measure a further 12in/300mm and mark the thread again. Pass the thread through the paper at the second reinforced point. Tie the thread around the spine at the second mark on the thread and cut off any spare. Find the first mark that you made on the thread, and tie a loop there to attach the flying line.*

# EDDY TRAIN

**DIFFICULTY:** INTERMEDIATE   **WIND:** MEDIUM – QUITE STRONG

## MATERIALS

Brown wrapping paper
10ft/3m × 30in/750mm
(or four pieces at least
30in/750mm square)

Eight pieces of ¼in/6mm
dowel, 28in/710mm long

Sticky tape

Acrylic paints, sponge and
plate for decoration

Strong glue

Scissors

Junior hacksaw

Crepe paper for tails

Strong thread or flying line

Water container in which
to soak dowelling (the
bath tub will do)

88lb/40kg flying line

## ALTERNATIVE MATERIALS

● These kites can be made
from any strong paper.

● The decoration can be
done using any thick
paint.

## ALTERNATIVE METHODS

● Strong thread can be
glued into the folded
edges of each kite to
give extra strength.

● The bridle point can be
adjusted to suit
different weather
conditions.

## FLYING TIPS

● In stronger winds these
kites can pull
surprisingly hard, so it is
important to wear
gloves made of leather
(or some other strong
material) to protect
your hands from line
burns.

● To launch the train,
release the kites one at
a time, starting with the
one furthest from the
flying line, and gradually
feed them into the sky.
It is extremely difficult
to launch kite trains
without assistance.

**1**

**2**

The Eddy Train described here consists of four kites strung together in a line. You can add more kites to the line as you become practised in flying them – several will fly just as well as one. Obviously you will need a stronger flying line as the number of kites increases, and extra reinforcement on the vulnerable areas of the kites may be needed.

**1** *Cut the ¼in/6mm dowel as necessary to make eight pieces 28in/710mm long. Four of these dowels will be spines; make a mark 5¼in/135mm from one end of each of these to indicate where the spars will intersect.*

**2** *Make a slit in the other end of each spine to a depth of ¼in/6mm (about the depth of a junior hacksaw blade). Be very careful with the saw – apply only gentle pressure and make sure that it does not slip and cut your hand.*

*The other four dowels will be cross-spars – mark the centre of each. Make a similar slit in both ends of all four cross-spars, making sure that both the slits are made in the same plane.*

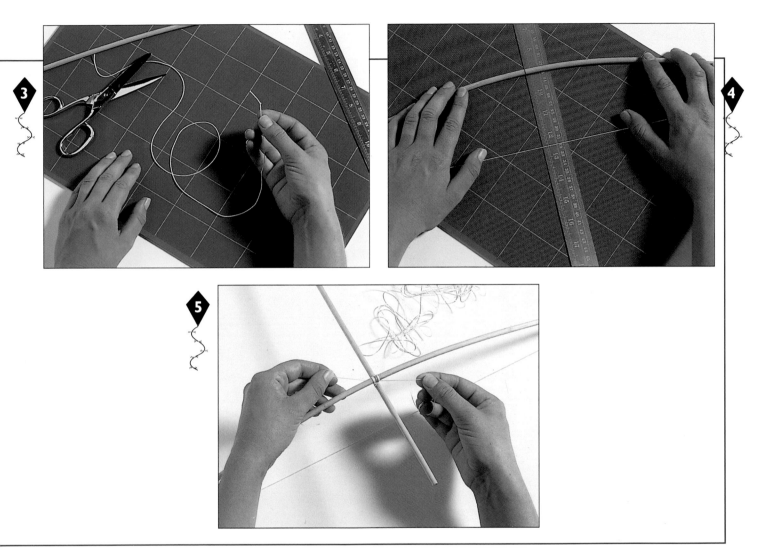

**3**

**4**

**5**

**3** Soak the four cross-spars under water for about two hours to make them more flexible.

Cut four 40in/1m lengths of strong line. Tie a knot near each end of all the pieces of line so that the knots are 26in/665mm apart.

**4** Slip the knoted line into the slit at one end of a soaked cross-spar. Bend the cross-spar carefully into a bow shape and slip the knot at the other end of the line into the other slit. The distance between the line and the centre of the bowed spar should be 3½in/90mm, and some adjustments may be necessary – check by measuring with a ruler.

Repeat the whole step with the other three cross-spars.

**5** Join pairs of spines and cross-spars at the centre marks by lashing the dowels together with strong line or thread and gluing for extra strength. Make sure that the two dowels are at right angles to each other with the bowed spar on top, as shown.

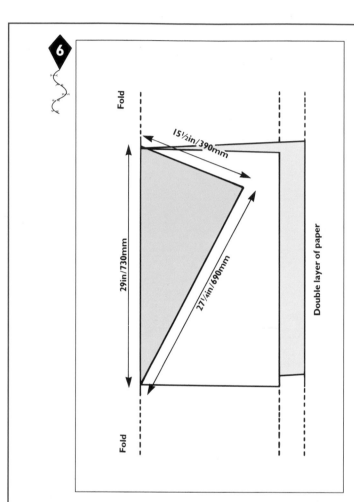

**6** *To make the sails, first fold the brown paper in half lengthways. Cut out four pieces to the dimensions shown in the diagram.*

**7** *Leave the paper folded, and cut out a small hole in each piece on the folded edge 5¾in/145mm down from the top point.*

**8** *Decorate the smooth side of the paper by printing a pattern with the sponge and paint (this step is, of course, optional).*

**9**

**10**

**11**

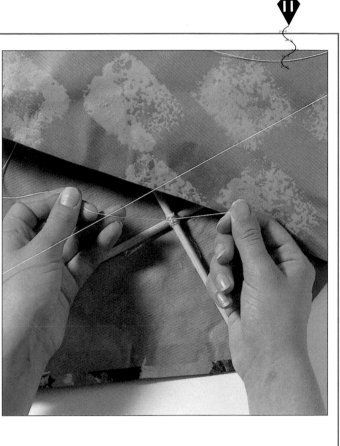

**9** *Fold in ⅜in/10mm of paper all round the edges towards the undecorated side, and trim off any excess on the corners. Fix the folded edges all round using sticky tape.*

**10** *Position the dowels on the back of the kite, with the spine against the sail and the cross-spar above the spine. The top of the spine should be flush with the top point of the sail – all the other spar ends should extend slightly beyond the edge of the paper. Stick the dowels onto the paper at intervals using sticky tape. Reinforce the points of the kite with extra sticky tape.*

**11** *When you have completed all four kites, join them together with strong line at the intersections of the spars. The kites should be about 6ft/1.8m apart. Knot the line at the intersection of the spars, thread through the hole in the sail and measure the distance to the next kite. The patterned sides of the four kites all face in the same direction.*

42

450mm
17³/₄in

29⁵/₈in/750mm

**12** *Join the kites together with a second line through the slit in the spar at the bottom of each kite. Tie the line around the stick and glue it for reinforcement. Make sure that the spacing of the kites remains even.*

**13** *Make the front bridle as shown in the diagram.*

**14** *Cut four pieces of crepe paper 3ft/900mm long and 2in/50mm wide for the tails. Snip a notch in the end of each piece and attach to the bottom of each kite with sticky tape either side of the spine.*

P R O J E C T   6

# D E L T A   B I R D

**DIFFICULTY:** INTERMEDIATE   **WIND:** LIGHT – MEDIUM

Scale: 1:5

Grain

Wings × 2

Keel × 1

Keel grain

Full size: 23½in/595mm

## MATERIALS

**Black ripstop nylon 39in/1m wide**

**Oddments of coloured ripstop nylon (for decoration)**

**Plastic tube to fit over dowels, 4¾in/120mm long**

**¼in/6mm dowel: two pieces 26in/660mm long for wings and one piece 22½in/575mm long for spine**

**½in/15mm dowel: one piece 30in/770mm long for spreader**

| | |
|---|---|
| **Ruler** | **Sandpaper** |
| **Glue stick** | **Strong thread** |
| **Scissors** | **22lb/10kg flying line** |
| **Craft knife** | |

## ALTERNATIVE MATERIALS

● **The dowelling may vary in thickness slightly without affecting the performance of the kite.**

The Delta Bird, as its name suggests, is very bird-like in flight – the kite will soar or hug the ground, and its wings flap. It is a very light-pulling kite, which requires a flying line of only 22lb/10kg.

**I** *Using squared paper, scale up the drawing (see page 19) and make a plain paper template to the finished size.*

**2**

**3**

**4**

**5**

45

**2** Fold the nylon and cut through both layers to produce two pieces to shape as shown. Pay careful attention to the direction of weave in the nylon, as marked on the template (step 1).

**3** Hem the edge of the keel with a single fold ⅜in/10mm wide. Use a fairly long stitch – about four stitches to ½in (three to 1cm) is best.

Cut a strip of nylon 2½in/60mm long × 1½in/40mm wide, fold the strip into three along its length and sew along the edges to form a narrow tab. Fold the tab in half across its width and sew it to the keel point to form a loop.

**4** Place the wing pieces right (top) sides together, with the keel sandwiched between them in the position shown on the template. Now sew the wings and keel together, stitching through all three pieces ¼in/6mm from the edge where they meet. Fold the wings back on each other (so that the keel is no longer between them), and press the seam out flat with a cool iron.

**5** Sew a seam joining the wings (but this time not the keel) ¾in/20mm in from the first line of stitching. Finish this seam ¾in/20mm from the bottom of the wing and strengthen with backstitches. Leave space for the spine to be fed through and continue stitching down and across the bottom of the section. Fit the spine dowel into the casing, trimming the dowel if necessary. Decorate with nylon and attach with glue on the side with the keel.

**6** *Sew the sleeving for the wing spars on the back of the kite, by making a ½in/15mm hem along the fronts of the wings, using a single fold. Sew across the top and bottom, leaving a gap to insert the wing spars.*

*Mark and carefully cut out a hole for the spreader attachment in the seam on each wing, taking care not to cut through the stitching. See template for the exact position of the hole.*

**7** *Cut two pieces of plastic tube, each 2½in/60mm long. Using a craft knife, make two small cross-cuts in each piece; the cuts should be about one quarter of the way along each piece, on opposing sides.*

**8** *Fit the wing dowels into the hems on the wings, threading them through the cross-cuts in the plastic tube. The tube should be at the centre of the slot in the hem.*

**9** *Fit the cross-spar into the plastic tubes across the back of the kite (the opposite side to the keel and decoration). The tubes will bend to give the wings some spring; in flight the wings will appear to flap. Tie the flying line onto the loop on the keel.*

# PROJECT 7
# SERPENT
**DIFFICULTY:** INTERMEDIATE  **WIND:** LIGHT – MEDIUM

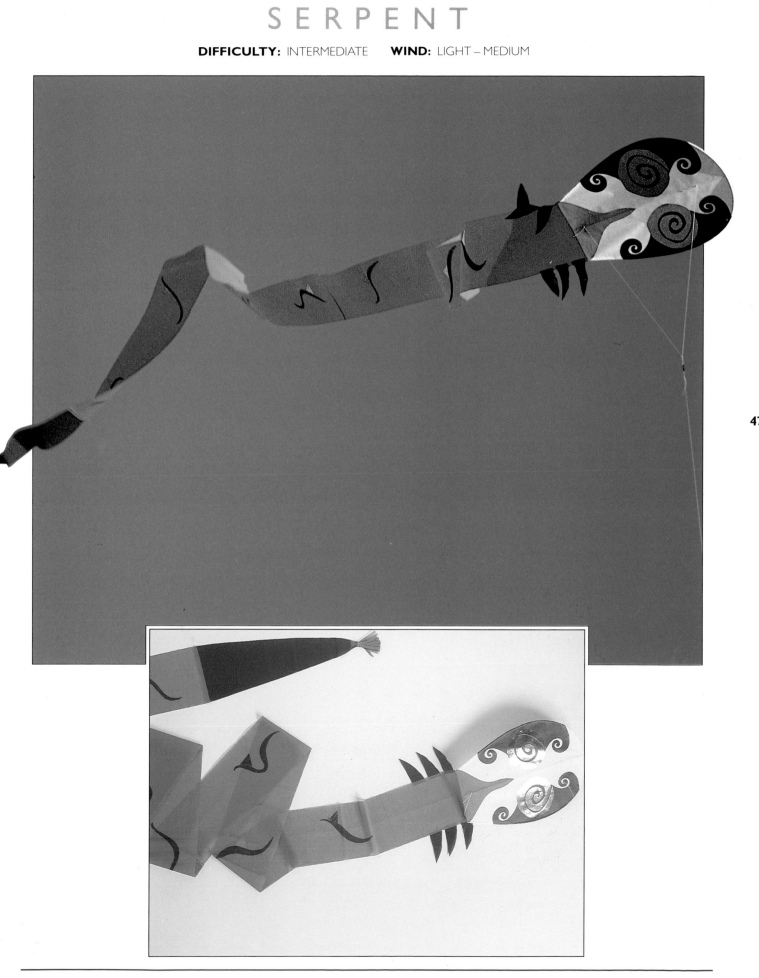

## MATERIALS

**Two pieces of paper – e.g., light cartridge – 23³⁄₈in/ 594mm × 16¹⁄₂in/420mm (A2 size)**

**Crepe paper of one colour, 20ft/6m long, for tail**

**Crepe paper of a second colour for decoration**

**Various coloured paper for decoration**

**60in/1.5m of ¹⁄₄in/6mm cane**

**20in/510mm of ¹⁄₄in/ 6mm dowel**

**Strong thread**

**Sticky tape**

**Glue stick**

**Spirit-based felt pen**

**Pencil**

**Scissors**

**Junior hacksaw**

**22lb/10kg flying line**

## ALTERNATIVE MATERIALS

● **This kite can be made using any light-weight paper or plastic.**

● **Bamboo sticks may be used for the spars.**

● **The colours of the sail and tail materials may, of course, be varied.**

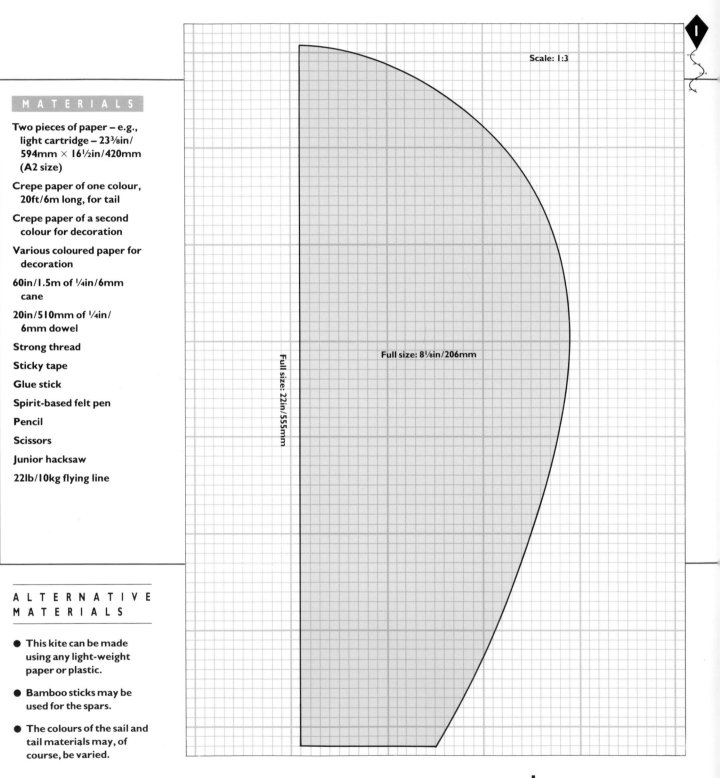

Scale: 1:3

Full size: 8¹⁄₈in/206mm

Full size: 22in/555mm

The serpent shape of this kite makes it great fun to fly – it is especially enjoyed by children. If the kite is going to be flown in heavier winds, it may be necessary to add length to the tail in order to improve its stability.

**I** *Copy the head template onto a folded piece of paper, scaling it up to full size (see page 19) and cut out the shape.*

**2** Put the pattern onto a sheet of kite paper that has been folded in half. The straight edge of the pattern sheet must align along the fold in the kite paper.

Using a pencil, draw around the pattern for the head on the folded kite paper. Cut with a pair of scissors along the line you have drawn.

**3** On the back of the kite, mark the two points at which you will attach the bridle. Both points should be on the fold line down the middle of the kite. One point should be 4½in/115mm from the top (curved edge) of the kite, the other 2½in/60mm from the bottom (straight edge). Reinforce these points using sticky tape or by gluing on patches of paper.

**4** Decorate the face of the kite using coloured markers and patches of coloured paper. Cut paper shapes with scissors and glue them on using a glue stick. A symmetrical pattern is best and, when paper is used, will not unbalance the kite. The easiest way to achieve symmetrical patterns is to cut them from paper folded in two.

**5** Cut a length of cane 49in/1.25m long (the short remaining piece will be needed later). Smooth the ends with sandpaper. Mark the centre of the cane.

50

**6** Mark three points on the kite: one ¾in/20mm from the top on the centre line; one in the bottom right corner, ¾in/20mm from the edges; one in the bottom left corner, ¾in/20mm from the edges.

**7** Using sticky tape, fix the centre of the cane to the point you have marked at the top of the kite.

**8** Bend the cane and fix the ends to the points you have marked in the bottom corners, again using sticky tape. Then use sticky tape to attach the other parts of the cane to the paper.

**9** Cut the shorter piece of cane so that it will fit between the ends of the curved cane. Then place it in position so that it is touching at both ends, and attach it with tape.

**10** *Using a hacksaw, cut the dowel to make the spine, which will run from the curved cane to the straight cane along the centre line of the kite. The dowel will need to be approximately 19⅝in/ 505mm long. Once it is cut to the correct length, fix the spine dowel in place with sticky tape.*

**11** *Using the sticky tape, reinforce the joints between all the spars.*

**12** *Fold the kite paper over the spars all around the edge and glue them in place using the glue stick.*

**13** *To make the tail, first cut a crepe paper strip the same width as the bottom of the kite and 20ft/6m long. Decorate it with felt pens and pieces of coloured paper. Attach this main part of the tail to the kite with tape.*

**14** Make six fin shapes of a contrasting colour. To do this, fold some crepe paper into six and cut out the shape. Stick three of the fins onto each side of the tail.

**15** Make a tassel by first cutting a strip of crepe paper about 20in/500mm wide and 4in/100mm deep. Then fold the paper along its length and, holding one end, snip to within 1/2in/15mm of the edge of the paper with scissors.

**16** Cut a strip of a different colour, the same width as the main strip at one end and tapering to a point at the other. Fix the wide end to the bottom end of the tail with glue. Attach the tassel to the point with sticky tape.

**17** Fix the bridle to the kite. The bridle, which should be 6ft/2 metres long, is tied around the spine dowel at the points you marked in step 3.

To find the point for the flying line to be attached, hold the bridle over your finger; when the wind lifts the kite to the appropriate angle, tie a loop in the bridle and fix the flying line to this. You should use line with at least 22lb/10kg breaking strain.

# DIAMOND STUNTER

**DIFFICULTY:** INTERMEDIATE     **WIND:** QUITE STRONG

This kite will perform gracefully once the flying technique has been mastered. The flying lines must be exactly the same length; once the kite is airborne pulling on both lines will cause the kite to rise, and using the left and right lines will produce sideways movement. With a little practice, the diamond stunter is great fun to fly and to watch.

## MATERIALS

- **Strong sheet of polythene or plastic bin bag**
- **Colourful plastic carrier bag for decoration and tail**
- **⅛in/3mm fibreglass rod, 35in/890mm long**
- **⅙in/4mm fibreglass rod, 33in/820mm long**
- **⅛-¼in/4–6mm reinforced plastic tube, 2in/50mm long**
- **Sticky tape**
- **Masking tape or insulating tape**
- **Craft knife or scissors**
- **Hacksaw**
- **Ruler**
- **Spirit-based marker pen**
- **Sandpaper**
- **6ft/2m strong line for bridle**
- **Two 22lb/10kg flying lines with handles**

## ALTERNATIVE MATERIALS

- This kite can be made from almost any non-stretchy polythene.

## ALTERNATIVE METHODS

- Removing the tail will make this kite even more responsive.

- If more robust materials are used, this kite can be bounced off the ground and will continue to fly.

- The lighter the kite is, the less wind it will need to fly successfully.

**2**

**3**

**4**

**1** *Fold the polythene in half and use a spirit-based felt pen to mark out the shape to the dimensions shown . Make sure the centre of the kite falls on the fold.*

**2** *Keep the polythene folded, and cut out the shape using a sharp craft knife or scissors.*

**3** *Unfold the polythene and mark the bridle points (see diagram). Reinforce the areas with sticky tape and pierce a hole in each.*

**4** *To make the corner pockets, fold flap A (see diagram) over and secure with sticky tape, then fold flap B over, stick down and reinforce with tape. Repeat on the other corner of the kite.*

**5** Cut two pieces of reinforced plastic tube 1in/ 25mm long. Attach one piece of these to the tab at the bottom of the kite with sticky tape.

**6** Roll the tube up in the tab. Make a cross-cut through the polythene and the tube with a sharp craft knife. This is to take the 1/6in/4mm fibreglass rod that will make the spine, and must be a tight fit, so it is better to make the cuts too small and enlarge them later if necessary.

**7** Roll the tube over so that the cross-cut faces the top of the kite. Fix the tube into place with sticky tape and reinforce well.

Now repeat steps 6 and 7 on the top of the kite, but this time finishing with the cross-cut facing downwards.

**8** Using a hacksaw, cut a length of 1/6in/4mm fibreglass rod to fit tightly between the top and bottom of the kite. This will be 33in/820mm long. Smooth the ends with sandpaper. Position the rod between the top and bottom tubes, making sure the ends fit snugly into the cross-cuts. Remove the spine again.

**9**

**10**

**11**

First loop

15in/380mm

15½in/390mm

**12**

**9** To make the cross-spar, cut a piece of ⅛in/3mm fibreglass rod about 35in/ 890mm long. Check before cutting that the spar will cross both bridle points; in order to do this it will have to bow slightly. Smooth any sharp ends and wrap them with a length of masking tape, folding the tape over the end to prevent the spar from piercing the sail.

**10** To make the bridle, first make a loop in the middle of 6ft/2m of line. Then make further loops in the positions shown in the diagram. The dimensions must be exactly the same on both sides of the kite.

**11** To fix the bridle to the kite, thread the loops through the sail onto the spine and cross-spar.

**12** Fix the spine and the cross-spar into position, with the cross-spar on top of the spine. The cross-spar will need to bow to fit into the corner pockets.

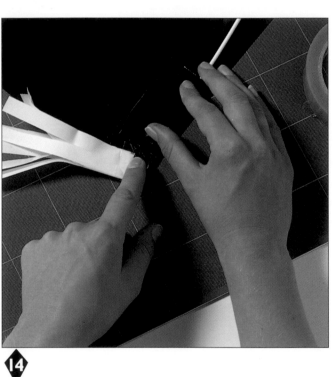

**13**

**14**

**13** To make the tail, cut a plastic carrier bag into 2in/50mm strips and stick them together, end to end, to make a length of about 18ft/6m. Reinforce the end of the tail with sticky tape, pierce a hole and thread it onto the spine (you will have to remove the spine from its socket to do this).

**14** Stick a short piece of plastic bag, folded once or twice and cut with scissors to make a fringe, onto each corner of the kite for decoration.

Tie on two flying lines of 22lb/10kg breaking strain to the bridle.

# PROJECT 9
# DELTA STUNTER

**DIFFICULTY:** MORE ADVANCED    **WIND:** MEDIUM – QUITE STRONG

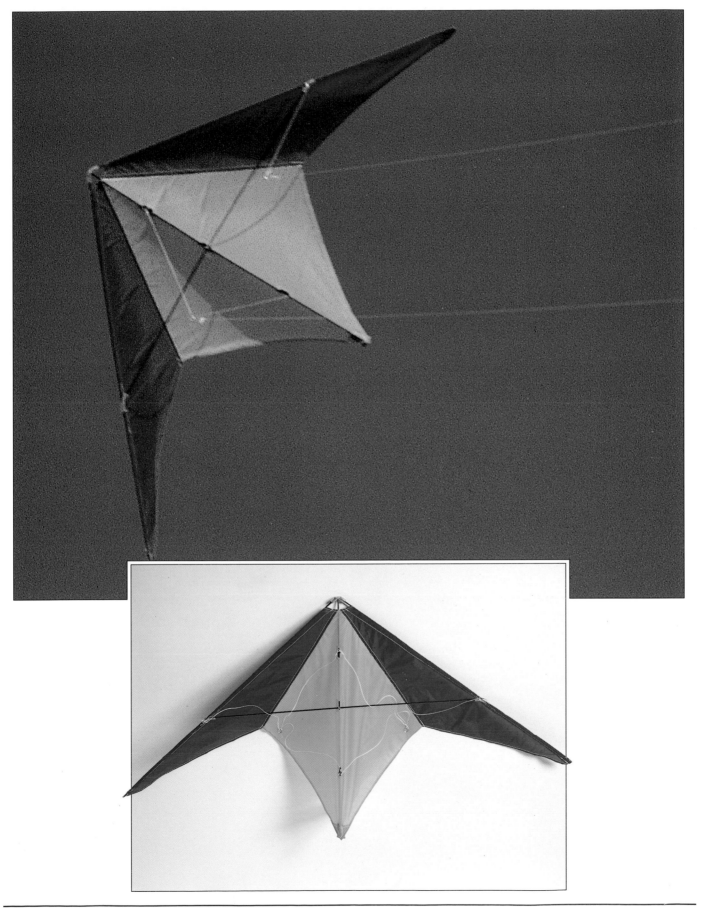

This kite can perform some spectacular stunts once you have mastered the flying technique, but do not practise in a crowded place, for safety reasons. The kite can be quite noisy when flown in stronger wind conditions. Small adjustments to the bridle may be necessary for effective flying.

## MATERIALS

**Red ripstop nylon 39in/1m square**

**Green ripstop nylon 39in/ 1m × 20in/500mm**

**¹⁄₈in/3.5mm carbon fibre rod: two pieces 36in/ 915mm long, one piece 30in/755mm long and one piece 33in/840mm long.**

**Reinforced plastic tube 5in/130mm long**

**Two ⁵⁄₈in/16mm split rings**

**Two rubber tap washers (to fit spine)**

**Strong braided line for bridles**

**Sticky tape**

**Double sided sticky tape**

**Extra strong thread**

**Insulating tape**

**Elastic band**

**Scissors**

**Craft knife**

**Junior hacksaw**

**88lb/40kg flying line and two handles**

## ALTERNATIVE MATERIALS

● **The carbon fibre rod can be replaced with a fibreglass rod or dowel, although the resulting kite will be less responsive. It is important that the spreader is fairly rigid.**

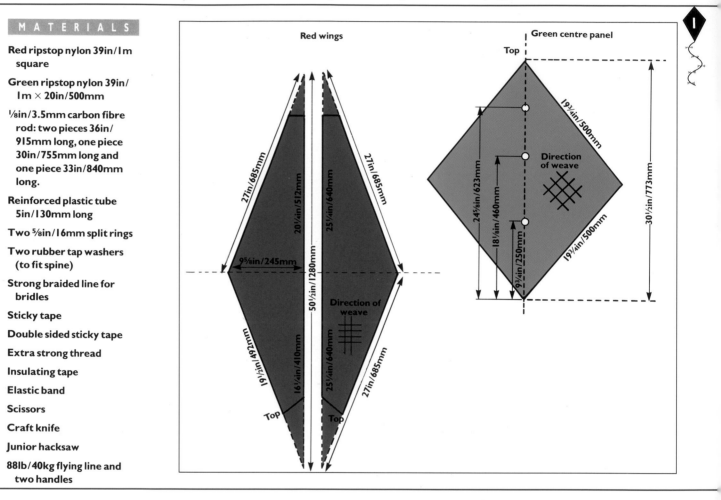

**I** *Cut the wings from the red nylon and the centre panel from the green nylon to the dimensions shown – be sure to note the direction of the fabric grain in each case.*

**2** *Fold the centre panel in half and mark the positions of the holes along the fold (see diagram to step 1). The holes will take the bridles when the kite is finished.*

**3** *To reinforce the holes, stick a piece of double sided tape onto a spare piece of nylon 1 1/2in/40mm long. Peel off the backing and stick it onto the back of the panel over the hole positions.*

**4** *Cut out the holes carefully with the panel folded in half.*

62

**5** *Sew a triangular reinforcement of green nylon to the back of the kite in the bottom corner of the centre panel.*

**6** *Make a double fold hem of ½in/15mm along the bottom edge of the centre panel. Make sure the hem falls on the back of the kite, and use a long stitch – about three stitches to ½in/1cm. Make a similar hem along the bottom edges of the red side panels.*

**7** *Join the red side panels to the centre green panel with a ½in/15mm seam on the back of the kite. The seams should end just short of the top of the kite.*

**8** *Fold the seam allowance over onto the red wing, and sew through all the layers onto the wing to make a neat flat seam as shown.*

**9** Neaten the seams and trim off any excess fabric. Fold ¼in/6mm of fabric over onto the back of the kite and stitch securely round the top of the kite. Fold in the side spar casing by ¾in/20mm and stitch near the edge.

**10** Fold in the wing tip by ½in/15mm. Turn the tips over once more by about 1⅛in/ 30mm and sew along the edges to form a pocket for the spars.

**11** Cut a piece of nylon 13in/330mm long × 1⅛in/ 30mm wide to make the bottom pocket. Fold the strip in half and in half again, and stitch to the back of the kite as shown.

**12** Make a semi-circular cut in each wing to accept the plastic tube for the cross-spar. Each cut-out should be about 2in/50mm long, and they must be symmetrical. The centre of the cut-out should be 14½in/370mm from the bottom wing tip. Reinforce the cut-outs with another row of stitching.

**13** Cut two pieces of reinforced plastic tube 1 ½in/ 40mm long. Slice a V-shaped notch in the centre of each piece of tube with a craft knife as shown. These will fit onto the wing spars to take the spreader.

**14** Cut a third piece of plastic tube 2in/50mm long and make a cross-cut in one side. This will be for the nose of the kite.

**15** Using a hacksaw, cut two wing spars 36in/915mm long from the carbon fibre rod. Wrap some insulating tape around one end of each spar so that they will fit the plastic nose tube tightly.

**16** Wrap some tape around each spar with the edge of the tape 14in/355mm from the untaped end.

**17** *Feed the wing spar through the sleeve on the wing from the top of the kite. The spar should pass through the plastic cross-spar connector at the cut-out in the hem and down to the wing tip. The tape wrapping on the spar will fit inside the tube when the spar is in position.*

**18** *From the carbon fibre rod, cut a piece 30in/755mm long for the spine. Wrap a strong elastic band around the middle of the spine. Wrap the spine with tape at the top and bottom, so that the edge of the tape is 6½in/165mm from the top and 8½in/215mm from the bottom. Trim the tap washers square and fit one onto each end of the spine outside the two taped places.*

**19** *Fit the bottom of the spine into the bottom pocket of the kite, and the top into the cross-cut of the plastic nose tube.*

**20** *Fit the wing spars into the nose tube, making sure that they fit tightly. Bending the nose tube down when you fit the spars will help to grip the spine.*

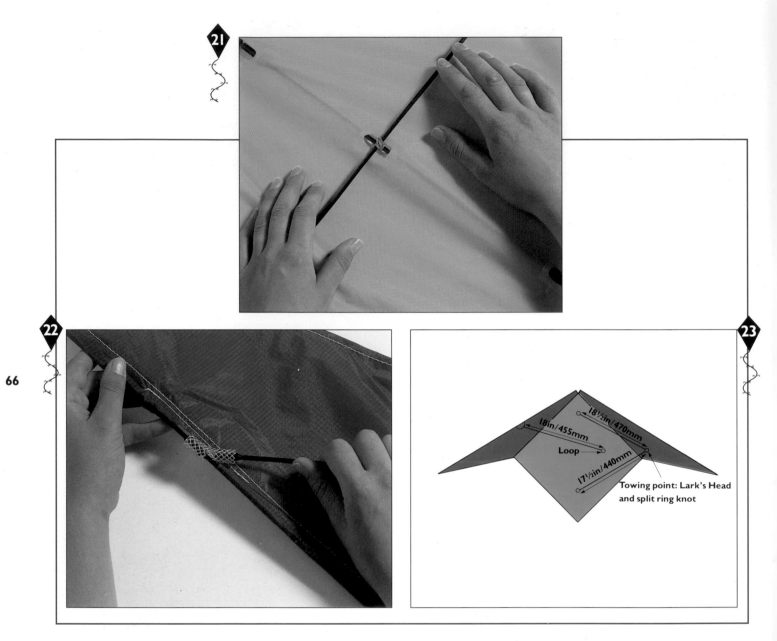

Loop

18in/455mm

18½in/470mm

17½in/440mm

**Towing point: Lark's Head and split ring knot**

**21** *From the carbon fibre rod, cut a piece 33in/840mm long for the spreader. Mark the centre point. With the spreader on the top of the kite, thread the spreader through the elastic band on the spine up to the centre mark.*

**22** *Wrap the ends of the spreader with insulating tape. Then fit the ends of the spreader into the tubes fixed to the wing spars. Make sure they fit tightly, adding more tape wrapping if necessary.*

**23** *Make two bridles, each of which has three legs. The diagram shows the construction of one of the bridles – the other should be a "mirror image" on the other side of the kite. You will need two pieces of line for each bridle. Note that the measurements given are for the finished bridle, after the knots have been tied. It's a good idea to mark the line clearly with a felt tip at the towing point. Attach a split ring to the towing point using a lark's head knot, before threading the loop of the outer leg onto the ring. When you have made both bridles, attach one flying line to each of the split rings.*

*To fine tune the kite, move the towing point slightly by loosening and adjusting the lark's head knot.*

# BOX KITE

**DIFFICULTY:** INTERMEDIATE   **WIND:** MEDIUM – QUITE STRONG

**1** 1¼in/30mm

12¼in/310mm

**2** 1¼in 30mm

3in 75mm

¼in/7.5mm

## MATERIALS

**Two strips of brown wrapping paper 50in/ 1270mm × 7in/180mm**

**Four pieces of ¼in/6mm dowel, 27in/680mm long**

**Four pieces of ¼in/6mm dowel, 16½in/422mm long**

**Plastic tube to fit over dowel, 9½in/240mm long**

**Sticky tape**

**Marker pens**

**Craft knife**

**Junior hacksaw**

**Scissors**

**33lb/15kg flying line**

## ALTERNATIVE MATERIALS

● **The box kite can be made from any type of strong paper.**

● **The thickness of the dowel and plastic tube can vary slightly if necessary.**

The box design of this kite gives it rigidity and strength, and the kite will be stable in flight even in quite strong wind conditions. Brown wrapping paper may seem an unassuming material to use, but it is surprisingly strong. At the end of a flying session, if great care is taken, the box kite can be collapsed down flat to make it easier to carry home.

**1** *Cut out two strips of paper 50in/1270mm × 7in/ 180mm. Fold the strips of paper as shown.*

**2** *Measure and mark with a pencil the position for holes on both of the folded edges. Make each hole 1⅛in/30mm wide and ¼in/7.5mm deep centred on the width of the paper. Unfold the paper and reinforce the places where holes will be cut using sticky tape on the back of the paper.*

**3** *Fold the paper again and cut out the holes through all the thicknesses – you will be cutting more than one hole at once.*

**4** *Decorate the front of the paper strips with marker pens.*

**5** *Cut four lengths of dowel 27in/680mm long. Smooth any rough ends with sandpaper. Measure and mark each piece of dowel ⅜in/ 10mm and 4¼in/110mm from both ends. These marks will serve to position the tubes that hold the cross-spars.*

**6** *Cut eight pieces of plastic tube 1⅛in/30mm long using the hacksaw. Slit each piece at the centre, taking care not to cut completely through the tube.*

**7** *Slide a piece of tube onto each end of each dowelling spar. The spars should pass into the end of the tube and exit through the slit you made in step 6. Line up the end of each tube with one of the marks on a spar. Make sure that both spurs of the tubes on each spar, face in the same direction.*

**8** Lay the spars onto the inside of one of the strips of the brownpaper, aligning each spar with a fold. The spars should extend ³⁄₈in/10mm beyond the edge of the paper and the tubes should be pointing upwards. Using sticky tape, fix the spars securely onto the paper.

Repeat with the other strip of paper, attaching it to the other ends of spars in the same way.

**9** Join the edges of both paper strips with sticky tape back and front, so that each forms a complete "band". The 1⅛in/30mm of paper in step 1 allows for an overlap.

**10** Cut four dowels to make cross-spars 16½in/ 422mm long. Smooth rough ends with sandpaper. Fit the cross-spars into the internal plastic tubes to brace the box. Take great care, as the paper is most liable to tear at this stage. The spars must be a good fit – if they are at all loose, wind some sticky tape around them; if they are too long, shorten them slightly until they fit. Reinforce all the joins between spars and paper with sticky tape.

**11** The flying line is tied directly onto the kite (no bridle is used). Pierce two small holes 5¾in/145mm down from the end of a corner spar, one on each side of the spar. Thread the flying line through one hole, round the spar, back through the other hole, and tie securely. Reinforce with sticky tape.

# STAR

**DIFFICULTY:** MORE ADVANCED   **WIND:** MEDIUM – QUITE STRONG

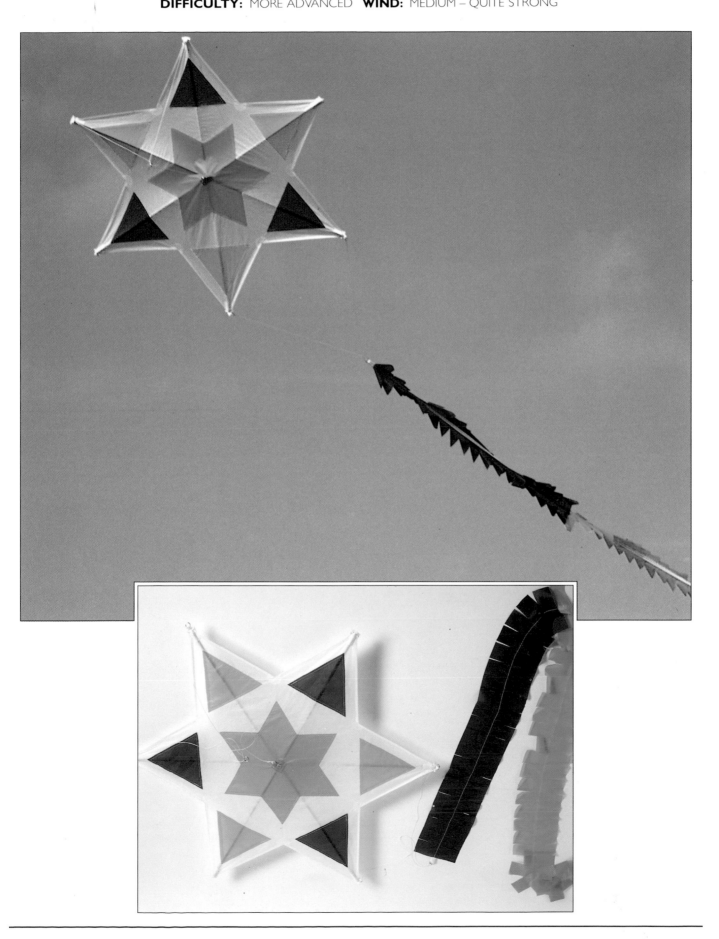

This colourful kite is fun to fly but will pull quite strongly even in moderate wind conditions – use a strong flying line and wear protective gloves to avoid line burns.

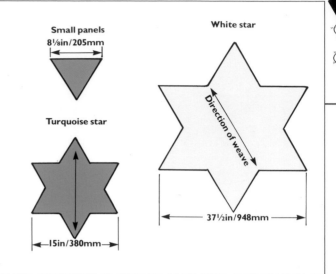

**Small panels**
8¹⁄₈in/205mm

**White star**

**Turquoise star**

Direction of weave

15in/380mm

37½in/948mm

## MATERIALS

**Plain white paper for templates**

**3ft/1m wide ripstop nylon in four colours: 4ft/1.25m of white, 3ft/1m of turquoise, 3ft/1m of purple; and 2ft 6in/0.75m of green**

**Seven ¹⁄₄in/6mm split rings**

**Three pieces of ³⁄₈in/9mm dowel, each 3ft/1m long**

**33ft/10m of strong fabric tape ¹⁄₂in/15mm wide**

**Strong thread or buttonhole thread and needle**

**Scissors**

**Junior hacksaw**

**Glue stick**

**Strong braided line for bridles**

**88lb/40kg flying line**

## ALTERNATIVE MATERIALS

● This kite can be made more simply by cutting out a hexagon shape instead of a star. Simply join the points of the star on the template with straight lines. The bridling remains the same.

● The kite can be made in one colour only, without the appliqué.

**1** *Draw the pattern onto plain paper and cut out. All the pieces are based on equilateral triangles. Fold the white nylon in half and use the pattern to cut out the star shape, noting the direction of the fabric grain. Mark the centre of the star. Cut out the turquoise star and mark the centre.*

**2** *Cut out the triangular decorative panels using the relevant patterns and colours. There are three green and three purple panels. The grain of each piece must match the grain of the white base. Stick the panels into position in the points of the star using glue stick around the edges. Stick the turquoise star into position, lining up the centre marks.*

**3** Stitch the coloured panels into place using a long stitch (about three stitches per ½in/10cm). Sew ¼in/6mm in from the edge of the panel, onto the front of the kite.

**4** On the back of the kite, cut away the white base behind each coloured panel ¼in/6mm in from the line of stitching.

**5** Cut six circles of nylon about 1¾in/45mm in diameter. Stitch the circles onto the back of the kite between the points as shown to act as reinforcement. Make a slit through both the reinforcement and the kite to the depth of the seam allowance, extending to the centre of the circle. This will make it easier to turn a hem at this point.

**6** Double fold a hem ½in/15mm deep all around the edges of the white star, and trim off any excess fabric at the points. Sew a double row of stitches over each circular patch to reinforce the edges.

74

**7** Cut a strip of turquoise nylon 6¼in/160mm long × 1½in/40mm wide. Fold the strip in half lengthwise, and then in half again. Sew it onto the centre of the back of the kite, using double rows of stitching.

　To make the centre back tie, cut a strip of white nylon 20in/500mm long × 1½in/40mm wide. Fold the strip into thirds along its length and sew along the edge. Sew the tie onto the back of the kite using double rows of stitching.

**8** To make the loops for the split rings, cut four strips of white nylon approximately 2¾in/70mm long × 1½in/40mm wide, and one strip of turquoise nylon to the same size. Fold each strip into thirds along its length and sew along the edge. Sew a white loop onto four points of the star, choosing two opposing pairs of points.

**9** Sew the turquoise loop made in step 8 onto the centre front of the kite using double rows of stitching. Thread a split ring onto all four white loops and the turquoise loop.

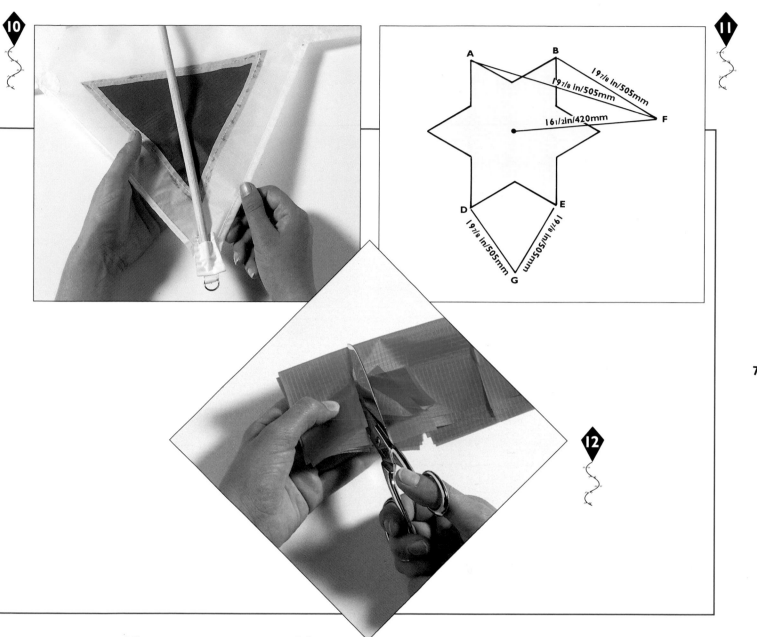

**10** *The diagram labels:* A, B, 19⅞ in/505mm, 19⅞ in/505mm, 16½ in/420mm, F, D, E, 19⅞ in/505mm, 19⅞ in/505mm, G

**10** *To make the star pockets, cut six strips of white nylon, 13in/330mm long × 1⅛in/30mm wide. Fold each strip in half and in half again, then double over and sew into place on each point of the star at the back of the kite using a double row of stitching around the edge. These pockets will take the ends of the spars when the kite is complete.*

**11** *Fix the bridle as shown in the diagram. A to B and D to E is a continuous length of braided line. Remember to allow extra for the take up on the loop. Thread split rings onto the loops at F and G. Check that the kite is evenly balanced by holding it at F.*

**12** *For the tail, cut 10 differently coloured strips of nylon 3ft/1m long × 6in/ 150mm wide. Fold the strips in half along their length, then into four across their width and snip along the unfolded side to make a fringe. Make each cut about 2in/50mm deep, and about 2in/50mm apart.*

**13** *Stitch the fringed strips along the centre onto a length of fabric tape, overlapping each colour slightly at the joins.*

**14** *Sew a loop at one end of the tape and fix the tail to the split ring at G (see diagram for step 11).*

**15** *Cut three pieces of ³⁄₈in/9mm dowel to about 3ft/1m long. Round off the ends with sandpaper.*

**16** *Fit the dowels across the star into the pockets. They should be a snug fit. The horizontal dowel will be especially tight as there is less stretch here on the grain of the fabric. Tie the dowels together with white nylon tie.*

# KEELED DIAMOND

**DIFFICULTY:** MORE ADVANCED **WIND:** MEDIUM – QUITE STRONG

78

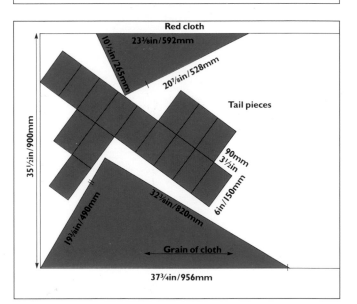

**MATERIALS**

Blue cotton poplin 35in/
90cm wide × 3ft/1m

Red cotton poplin to the
same size

³⁄₈in/9mm dowel, 6ft/2m
long

¹⁄₂in/15mm wide tape,
18ft/6m long

1¹⁄₄in/32mm Petersham
(or wide tape), 18in/
450mm long

Strong thread and needles

Two ¹⁄₄in/6mm eyelets and
a punch (or equivalent)
for fixing (optional)

Fishing swivel clip
(optional)

Junior hacksaw

Scissors

Sandpaper

Pencil or tailor's chalk

44lb/20kg flying line

**ALTERNATIVE
MATERIALS**

● The sail can be made
from any densely woven
cloth that is not liable to
stretch too much – e.g.,
sheeting or lining.

● Thinner dowel can be
used if necessary.

● The pockets can be made
of any thick tape.

● Tape loops can be used
instead of the eyelets.

**ALTERNATIVE
METHODS**

● Although a flat fell seam
is recommended for
neatness and strength,
you can simply stitch the
cloth together leaving the
raw edges at the back of
the kite. The more rows
of stitching you use, the
less the kite will stretch.
Another alternative is to
stitch tape over the
seams.

This two-tone kite with its tail of bows is very traditional in
shape. The length of the kite's tail will need to vary
depending on the wind conditions; stronger winds need a
longer tail. The flying line can also be moved from the top
eyelet (for light winds) to the lower one (for stronger winds).

**1** *Make paper templates for
each colour as shown in the
diagrams. Place the templates
on the right colour cloth,
making sure the direction of
the weave is correct. Mark the
outlines in pencil or tailor's
chalk and cut out carefully.
You will have two red and two
blue triangles for the kite
body, and a narrow blue
triangle for the keel.*

**2** Cut a piece of ½in/15mm wide tape to 3½in/90mm long, and trim it to match the shape of the keel at the towing point. Allow ½in/15mm from the edge of the keel for a hem. Sew the tape into position along two sides.

**3** Hem along two edges of the keel with a double fold, turning over ½in/15mm in total. Mark two points on the reinforced part of the keel 2in/50mm apart as shown, and punch an eyelet into each (alternatively, attach a tape loop) for the flying line. Take care not to perforate the stitching.

**4** Sew a small triangle to a contrasting large one, to form one half of the sail, using a flat fell seam for strength and neatness. Repeat for the other half of the sail. Place the two halves right sides together, and position the keel between them, 2½in/60mm from the top of the kite. Trim one side of the seam allowances to reduce the bulk of the seam and flat fell the keel into place. Hem all round the kite using a double fold ½in/15mm wide.

**5** For the pockets, cut four pieces of 1¼in/32mm wide Petersham, or tape, to a length of 2½in/60mm, and fold each piece as shown. Stitch a pocket onto the bottom of the kite, placing a loop of tape between the kite and pocket to take the tail, using a double row of stitching all round the pocket.

**6** Stitch pockets onto the other three points of the kite, trimming off any fabric that extends beyond the edge of the kite. These three pockets do not need loops.

**7** Cut two pieces of dowel that will fit the kite snugly, and round off any sharp ends with sandpaper.

**8** Cut two pieces of narrow tape 20in/500mm long. Stitch the tapes onto the back of the kite at the junction of the two spars and at a point 14in/350mm further down. Tie the tapes over the spar and the spine.

**9** To make the tail, cut 15 red and 15 blue pieces of fabric 3½in/90mm × 6in/150mm. Cut on the cross grain of the fabric to lessen the risk of fraying. Pin alternate colours onto the narrow tape at 8in/200mm intervals, ruching each piece to make a bow shape, and stitch securely into place.

**10** A fishing swivel hook sewn onto the end of the tail will help to prevent it knotting up in the air. Alternatively, the tail can simply be tied onto the loop at the bottom of the kite.

Attach the flying line to one of the eyelets in the keel (the top for lighter winds and the bottom for stronger).